THIS ADDRESS BOOK
BELONGS TO

NAME...

....

ADDRESS..

....

....

....

TEL...

FAX...

E-MAIL..

ADDRESS BOOK

ANTIQUE COLLECTORS' CLUB

ISBN 1 85149 417 0

British Library Cataloguing-in-Publication Data
A catalogue record for this book is available from the British Library

FRONT COVER: Percival Leonard Rosseau, *Leda* (detail), 1906

BACK COVER: Malcolm S. Tucker, *Dog with a Ball*, 1893

FRONTISPIECE: Barrie Barnett, *Jay*

TITLE PAGE: George Earl, *Prince*, c.1870

ENDPAPER: Richard Ansdell, *Highland Tod, Foxhunter*, 1859

Printed in England by the Antique Collectors' Club Ltd., Woodbridge, Suffolk IP12 4SD

The works of art illustrated in this book come from the collections of The American Kennel Club and The American Kennel Club Museum of The Dog. They represent a selection of the four hundred color illustrations featured in *A Breed Apart*, by William Secord, and published by the Antique Collectors' Club.

The American Kennel Club was founded in 1884 and has become America's primary registry for purebred dogs. It registers in excess of one million purebred dogs each year, and is the nation's leading not-for-profit organization devoted to the study, breeding, exhibiting and advancement of purebred dogs.

The American Kennel Club Museum of the Dog was founded in 1981 to collect, preserve and exhibit, works of art, books and artifacts on the dog. Over the years, it has amassed a large collection and is open to the public on a regular basis. The Museum also hosts special educational programs for children and maintains a reference library.

THE AMERICAN KENNEL CLUB
260 Madison Avenue
New York
NY 10016, USA
Tel: 212-696-8200
Fax: 212-696-8299
www.akc.org

THE AKC MUSEUM OF THE DOG
1721 South Mason Road
St. Louis
MO 63131, USA
Tel: 314-821-3647
Fax: 314-821-7381

ANTIQUE COLLECTORS' CLUB
Martlesham
Woodbridge
Suffolk, IP12 4SD, UK
Tel: 01394 389950
Fax: 01394 389999
www.antique-acc.com

IMPORTANT TELEPHONE NUMBERS

VET... ....

DOCTOR.. ....

DENTIST... ....

POLICE.. ....

ELECTRICITY.. ....

WATER.. ....

GAS... ....

TELEPHONE ....

BANK.. ....

CREDIT CARD LOSS............................... ....

INSURANCE... ....

SOLICITOR.. ....

BUILDER... ....

PLUMBER.. ....

ELECTRICIAN.. ....

GARAGE.. ....

TAXI.. ....

....

....

A

NAME..

ADDRESS..

....

....

TEL ....
FAX..
E-MAIL...

NAME..

ADDRESS..

....

....

TEL ....
FAX..
E-MAIL...

Edwin Megargee, *Ch. Basquaerie Marsous*, c.1937

A

Edwin Megargee,
Standing St. Bernard

NAME...

ADDRESS ....

....

....

TEL ....
FAX ....
E-MAIL ....

NAME...

ADDRESS ....

....

....

TEL ....
FAX ....
E-MAIL ....

NAME...

ADDRESS ....

....

....

TEL ....
FAX ....
E-MAIL ....

NAME...

ADDRESS ....

....

....

TEL ....
FAX ....
E-MAIL ....

A

NAME...

ADDRESS ....

....

....

....

TEL ....

FAX..

E-MAIL...

NAME...

ADDRESS ....

....

....

....

TEL ....

FAX..

E-MAIL...

NAME...

ADDRESS ....

....

....

....

TEL ....

FAX..

E-MAIL...

NAME...

ADDRESS ....

....

....

....

TEL ....

FAX..

E-MAIL...

NAME...

ADDRESS ....

....

....

....

TEL ....

FAX..

E-MAIL...

Edwin Megargee, *Briard*

Frederick Thomas Daws, *Ch. Queen of Lyons*, 1923

NAME..

ADDRESS..

....

....

TEL..

FAX..

E-MAIL..

NAME..

ADDRESS..

....

....

TEL..

FAX..

E-MAIL..

NAME..

ADDRESS..

....

....

TEL..

FAX..

E-MAIL..

NAME..

ADDRESS..

....

....

TEL..

FAX..

E-MAIL..

NAME..

ADDRESS..

....

....

TEL..

FAX..

E-MAIL..

A

NAME......................................

ADDRESS................................

....

....

TEL ....
FAX..
E-MAIL..................................

NAME......................................

ADDRESS................................

....

....

TEL ....
FAX..
E-MAIL..................................

NAME......................................

ADDRESS................................

....

....

TEL ....
FAX..
E-MAIL..................................

NAME......................................

ADDRESS................................

....

....

TEL ....
FAX..
E-MAIL..................................

Marguerite Kirmse, *Under the Mistletoe*, 1935

A

NAME..

....

ADDRESS...

....

....

....

TEL...

FAX..

E-MAIL...

NAME..

....

ADDRESS...

....

....

TEL...

FAX..

E-MAIL...

NAME..

....

ADDRESS...

....

....

....

TEL...

FAX..

E-MAIL...

NAME..

....

ADDRESS...

....

....

TEL...

FAX..

E-MAIL...

Herbert Dicksee, *Sleeping French Bulldog*

NAME..

....

ADDRESS...

....

....

....

TEL...

FAX..

E-MAIL...

NAME...

ADDRESS...

....

....

TEL ....
FAX..
E-MAIL...

NAME...

ADDRESS...

....

....

TEL ....
FAX..
E-MAIL...

NAME...

ADDRESS...

....

....

TEL ....
FAX..
E-MAIL...

NAME...

ADDRESS...

....

....

TEL ....
FAX..
E-MAIL...

NAME...

ADDRESS...

....

....

TEL ....
FAX..
E-MAIL...

Persis Kirmse, *Ch. Broadway Admiration*, c.1920

B

NAME...

ADDRESS...

....

....

TEL..

FAX...

E-MAIL..

NAME...

ADDRESS...

....

....

TEL..

FAX...

E-MAIL..

NAME...
....
ADDRESS..
....
....
....
TEL ....
FAX...
E-MAIL..

NAME...
....
ADDRESS..
....
....
....
TEL ....
FAX...
E-MAIL..

Nevison Arthur Loraine, *Mouton*, 1892

Left: Malcolm S. Tucker, *Dog with a Ball*, 1893

NAME...
....
ADDRESS..
....
....
....
TEL ....
FAX...
E-MAIL..

NAME...
....
ADDRESS..
....
....
....
TEL ....
FAX...
E-MAIL..

B

NAME...

ADDRESS..

....

....

TEL..
FAX..
E-MAIL...

NAME...

ADDRESS..

....

....

TEL..
FAX..
E-MAIL...

NAME...

ADDRESS..

....

....

TEL..
FAX..
E-MAIL...

NAME...

ADDRESS..

....

....

TEL..
FAX..
E-MAIL...

NAME...

ADDRESS..

....

....

TEL..
FAX..
E-MAIL...

NAME...

ADDRESS..

....

....

TEL..
FAX..
E-MAIL...

NAME..

ADDRESS..

....

....

TEL...
FAX...
E-MAIL...

NAME..

ADDRESS..

....

....

TEL...
FAX...
E-MAIL...

Gustav Muss-Arnolt, *Ch. Windholme's Roadster*, 1903

NAME..

ADDRESS..

....

....

TEL...
FAX...
E-MAIL...

NAME..

ADDRESS..

....

....

TEL...
FAX...
E-MAIL...

B

NAME...

ADDRESS..

....

....

TEL...
FAX...
E-MAIL...

NAME...

ADDRESS..

....

....

TEL...
FAX...
E-MAIL...

NAME...

ADDRESS..

....

....

TEL...
FAX...
E-MAIL...

NAME...

ADDRESS..

....

....

TEL...
FAX...
E-MAIL...

NAME...

ADDRESS..

....

....

TEL...
FAX...
E-MAIL...

NAME...

ADDRESS..

....

....

TEL...
FAX...
E-MAIL...

B

A.S., Mr. J. Royle's *Distinguished Champions of the Show Bench*, 1888

B

NAME..

ADDRESS...

....

....

....

TEL...
FAX...
E-MAIL...

NAME..

ADDRESS...

....

....

....

TEL...
FAX...
E-MAIL...

NAME..

ADDRESS...

....

....

....

TEL...
FAX...
E-MAIL...

NAME..

ADDRESS...

....

....

....

TEL...
FAX...
E-MAIL...

NAME..

ADDRESS...

....

....

....

TEL...
FAX...
E-MAIL...

NAME..

ADDRESS...

....

....

....

TEL...
FAX...
E-MAIL...

C

NAME...

ADDRESS..

....

....

TEL ....
FAX...
E-MAIL...

NAME...

ADDRESS..

....

....

TEL ....
FAX...
E-MAIL...

NAME...

ADDRESS..

....

....

TEL ....
FAX...
E-MAIL...

NAME...

ADDRESS..

....

....

TEL ....
FAX...
E-MAIL...

NAME...

ADDRESS..

....

....

TEL ....
FAX...
E-MAIL...

Frank Paton, *Greyhound*

C

Emmanuel Frémiet, *Ravageot and Ravageole*

NAME...

ADDRESS...

....

....

....

TEL...
FAX..
E-MAIL...

NAME...

ADDRESS...

....

....

....

TEL...
FAX..
E-MAIL...

NAME...

ADDRESS...

....

....

....

TEL...
FAX..
E-MAIL...

NAME...

ADDRESS...

....

....

....

TEL...
FAX..
E-MAIL...

NAME...
....
ADDRESS...
....
....
....
TEL ....
FAX...
E-MAIL...

NAME...
....
ADDRESS...
....
....
....
TEL ....
FAX...
E-MAIL...

H.-A.-M. Jacquemart, *Mastiff Seated with Turtle*

NAME...
....
ADDRESS...
....
....
....
TEL ....
FAX...
E-MAIL...

NAME...
....
ADDRESS...
....
....
....
TEL ....
FAX...
E-MAIL...

C

NAME..

....

ADDRESS..

....

....

....

TEL...

FAX...

E-MAIL...

NAME..

....

ADDRESS..

....

....

....

TEL...

FAX...

E-MAIL...

NAME..

ADDRESS..

....

....

....

TEL ....

FAX..

E-MAIL...

NAME..

ADDRESS..

....

....

....

TEL ....

FAX..

E-MAIL...

Paul-Édouard Delabrièrre, *Two Chained Mastiffs*

Left: Georges Gardet, *Recumbent Great Dane*, 1880

NAME..

ADDRESS..

....

....

....

TEL ....

FAX..

E-MAIL...

NAME..

ADDRESS..

....

....

....

TEL ....

FAX..

E-MAIL...

C

NAME..

ADDRESS...

....

....

....

TEL...
FAX...
E-MAIL...

NAME..

ADDRESS...

....

....

....

TEL...
FAX...
E-MAIL...

NAME..

ADDRESS...

....

....

....

TEL...
FAX...
E-MAIL...

NAME..

ADDRESS...

....

....

....

TEL...
FAX...
E-MAIL...

NAME..

ADDRESS...

....

....

....

TEL...
FAX...
E-MAIL...

NAME..

ADDRESS...

....

....

....

TEL...
FAX...
E-MAIL...

D

Arthur Batt, *Horse, Mastiff and Newfoundland*, 1881

NAME..

ADDRESS..

....

....

....

TEL ....

FAX..

E-MAIL..

NAME..

ADDRESS..

....

....

....

TEL ....

FAX..

E-MAIL..

D

NAME...

ADDRESS ....

....

....

....

TEL ....

FAX..

E-MAIL..

NAME...

ADDRESS ....

....

....

....

TEL ....

FAX..

E-MAIL..

NAME...

ADDRESS ....

....

....

....

TEL ....

FAX..

E-MAIL..

NAME...

ADDRESS ....

....

....

....

TEL ....

FAX..

E-MAIL..

D

NAME..
....
ADDRESS..
....
....
....
TEL ....
FAX..
E-MAIL..

NAME..
....
ADDRESS..
....
....
....
TEL ....
FAX..
E-MAIL..

NAME..
....
ADDRESS..
....
....
....
TEL ....
FAX..
E-MAIL..

John Thomas Peele, *Waiting for Their Master*

Left: Gustav Muss-Arnolt, *Real English*

D

Above and right: Gustav Muss-Arnolt, *Standing Borzois*

NAME...

ADDRESS...

....

....

....

TEL ....

FAX..

E-MAIL..

NAME...

ADDRESS...

....

....

....

TEL ....

FAX..

E-MAIL..

NAME...

ADDRESS...

....

....

....

TEL ....

FAX..

E-MAIL..

NAME...

ADDRESS...

....

....

....

TEL ....

FAX..

E-MAIL..

D

NAME..

ADDRESS ....

....

....

....

TEL ....
FAX...
E-MAIL...

NAME..

ADDRESS ....

....

....

....

TEL ....
FAX...
E-MAIL...

NAME..

ADDRESS ....

....

....

....

TEL ....
FAX...
E-MAIL...

NAME..

ADDRESS ....

....

....

....

TEL ....
FAX...
E-MAIL...

NAME..

ADDRESS ....

....

....

....

TEL ....
FAX...
E-MAIL...

E

NAME...

ADDRESS..

....

....

....

TEL...

FAX..

E-MAIL...

NAME...

ADDRESS..

....

....

TEL...

FAX..

E-MAIL...

NAME...

ADDRESS..

....

....

TEL...

FAX..

E-MAIL...

NAME...

ADDRESS..

....

....

TEL...

FAX..

E-MAIL...

NAME...

ADDRESS..

....

....

TEL...

FAX..

E-MAIL...

E

NAME...

ADDRESS ....

....

....

....

TEL ....

FAX...

E-MAIL..

NAME...

ADDRESS ....

....

....

....

TEL ....

FAX...

E-MAIL..

Left: Percival Leonard
Rosseau, *Setter in a Field*, 1900

Edwin Frederick Holt,
In Times of Peace, 1877

E

NAME..

....

ADDRESS ....

....

....

....

TEL ....

FAX..

E-MAIL..

NAME..

....

ADDRESS ....

....

....

....

TEL ....

FAX..

E-MAIL..

NAME..

....

ADDRESS ....

....

....

....

TEL ....

FAX..

E-MAIL..

NAME..

....

ADDRESS ....

....

....

....

TEL ....

FAX..

E-MAIL..

Percival Leonard Rosseau, *Head Studies of Borzois*, 1911

NAME...

ADDRESS ....

....

....

TEL ....

FAX...

E-MAIL..

NAME...

ADDRESS ....

....

....

TEL ....

FAX...

E-MAIL..

Gustav Muss-Arnolt, *Wan Lung*

NAME...

ADDRESS ....

....

....

TEL ....

FAX...

E-MAIL..

NAME...

ADDRESS ....

....

....

TEL ....

FAX...

E-MAIL..

F

NAME...

ADDRESS..

....

....

TEL ....
FAX..
E-MAIL..

NAME...

ADDRESS..

....

....

TEL ....
FAX..
E-MAIL..

NAME...
....
ADDRESS...
....
....
....
TEL ....
FAX...
E-MAIL..

NAME...
....
ADDRESS...
....
....
....
TEL ....
FAX...
E-MAIL..

John Emms, *Richmond Jack*, 1881

Left: John Emms, *Two Foxhounds and Fox Terrier on a Kennel Bench*

NAME...
....
ADDRESS...
....
....
....
TEL ....
FAX...
E-MAIL..

NAME...
....
ADDRESS...
....
....
....
TEL ....
FAX...
E-MAIL..

F

NAME...

ADDRESS...

....

....

TEL..
FAX..
E-MAIL...

NAME...

ADDRESS...

....

....

TEL..
FAX..
E-MAIL...

NAME...

ADDRESS...

....

....

TEL..
FAX..
E-MAIL...

NAME...

ADDRESS...

....

....

TEL..
FAX..
E-MAIL...

NAME...

ADDRESS...

....

....

TEL..
FAX..
E-MAIL...

NAME...

ADDRESS...

....

....

TEL..
FAX..
E-MAIL...

F

NAME..
....
ADDRESS..
....
....
....
TEL ....
FAX...
E-MAIL...

NAME..
....
ADDRESS..
....
....
....
TEL ....
FAX...
E-MAIL...

John Henry Frederick Bacon, *Maud, Daughter of Colonel Temple with her two Schipperkes*, 1899

NAME..
....
ADDRESS..
....
....
....
TEL ....
FAX...
E-MAIL...

NAME..
....
ADDRESS..
....
....
....
TEL ....
FAX...
E-MAIL...

F

NAME..

ADDRESS..

....

....

....

TEL...
FAX...
E-MAIL...

NAME..

ADDRESS..

....

....

....

TEL...
FAX...
E-MAIL...

NAME..

ADDRESS..

....

....

....

TEL...
FAX...
E-MAIL...

NAME..

ADDRESS..

....

....

....

TEL...
FAX...
E-MAIL...

NAME..

ADDRESS..

....

....

....

TEL...
FAX...
E-MAIL...

NAME..

ADDRESS..

....

....

....

TEL...
FAX...
E-MAIL...

Maud Earl,
I Hear a Voice, 1896

NAME...

ADDRESS..

....

....

....

TEL ....

FAX...

E-MAIL...

NAME...

ADDRESS..

....

....

....

TEL ....

FAX...

E-MAIL...

G

Maud Earl, *Silent Sorrow*, 1910

NAME..

ADDRESS...

....

....

TEL ....
FAX..
E-MAIL..

NAME..

ADDRESS...

....

....

TEL ....
FAX..
E-MAIL..

NAME..

ADDRESS...

....

....

TEL ....
FAX..
E-MAIL..

NAME..

ADDRESS...

....

....

TEL ....
FAX..
E-MAIL..

G

NAME..
....
ADDRESS..
....
....
....
TEL ....
FAX...
E-MAIL..

NAME..
....
ADDRESS..
....
....
....
TEL ....
FAX...
E-MAIL..

NAME..
....
ADDRESS..
....
....
....
TEL ....
FAX...
E-MAIL..

NAME..
....
ADDRESS..
....
....
....
TEL ....
FAX...
E-MAIL..

NAME..
....
ADDRESS..
....
....
....
TEL ....
FAX...
E-MAIL..

Maud Earl, *A Ruling From the Chair*, 1903

G

NAME..

ADDRESS..

....

....

....

TEL..
FAX..
E-MAIL..

NAME..

ADDRESS..

....

....

....

TEL..
FAX..
E-MAIL..

NAME..

ADDRESS..

....

....

....

TEL..
FAX..
E-MAIL..

NAME..

ADDRESS..

....

....

....

TEL..
FAX..
E-MAIL..

NAME..

ADDRESS..

....

....

....

TEL..
FAX..
E-MAIL..

NAME..

ADDRESS..

....

....

....

TEL..
FAX..
E-MAIL..

G

Christine Merrill, *Millie on the South Lawn*, 1990

H

NAME..

ADDRESS..

....

....

....

TEL..

FAX...

E-MAIL...

NAME..

ADDRESS..

....

....

....

TEL..

FAX...

E-MAIL...

NAME..

ADDRESS..

....

....

....

TEL..

FAX...

E-MAIL...

NAME..

ADDRESS..

....

....

....

TEL..

FAX...

E-MAIL...

NAME..

ADDRESS..

....

....

....

TEL..

FAX...

E-MAIL...

NAME..

ADDRESS..

....

....

....

TEL..

FAX...

E-MAIL...

NAME..

ADDRESS..

....

....

TEL...
FAX...
E-MAIL...

Amy Gessner Larson, *Penn Marydell Pandemonium*, 1988

NAME..

ADDRESS..

....

....

TEL...
FAX...
E-MAIL...

NAME..

ADDRESS..

....

....

TEL...
FAX...
E-MAIL...

NAME..

ADDRESS..

....

....

TEL...
FAX...
E-MAIL...

H

Marion Needham Krupp 1988

NAME..
....
ADDRESS...
....
....
....
TEL...
FAX...
E-MAIL...

NAME..
....
ADDRESS...
....
....
....
TEL...
FAX...
E-MAIL...

NAME..
....
ADDRESS...
....
....
....
TEL...
FAX...
E-MAIL...

NAME..
....
ADDRESS...
....
....
....
TEL...
FAX...
E-MAIL...

NAME..

ADDRESS...

....

....

TEL ....

FAX..

E-MAIL...

NAME..

ADDRESS...

....

....

TEL ....

FAX..

E-MAIL...

Roy Andersen, *Ch. Kay's Don Feleciano-L*, 1986

Left: Marion Needham Krupp, *Couch Scottie*, c.1988

NAME..

ADDRESS...

....

....

....

TEL ....

FAX..

E-MAIL...

NAME..

ADDRESS...

....

....

....

TEL ....

FAX..

E-MAIL...

H

NAME..

ADDRESS..

....

....

TEL..
FAX..
E-MAIL...

NAME..

ADDRESS..

....

....

TEL..
FAX..
E-MAIL...

NAME..

ADDRESS..

....

....

TEL..
FAX..
E-MAIL...

NAME..

ADDRESS..

....

....

TEL..
FAX..
E-MAIL...

NAME..

ADDRESS..

....

....

TEL..
FAX..
E-MAIL...

NAME..

ADDRESS..

....

....

TEL..
FAX..
E-MAIL...

H

NAME...

....

ADDRESS..

....

....

....

TEL ....

FAX..

E-MAIL...

NAME...

....

ADDRESS..

....

....

....

TEL ....

FAX..

E-MAIL...

Donald Grant, *Saluki Studies*

I

NAME

ADDRESS

TEL
FAX
E-MAIL

NAME

ADDRESS

TEL
FAX
E-MAIL

NAME

ADDRESS

TEL
FAX
E-MAIL

NAME

ADDRESS

TEL
FAX
E-MAIL

NAME

ADDRESS

TEL
FAX
E-MAIL

NAME

ADDRESS

TEL
FAX
E-MAIL

Roy Andersen,
The Beat of Wings, 1984

NAME..

....

ADDRESS...

....

....

....

TEL...

FAX..

E-MAIL...

NAME..

....

ADDRESS...

....

....

....

TEL...

FAX..

E-MAIL...

J

NAME...

ADDRESS...
....
....
....

TEL ....
FAX..
E-MAIL...

NAME...

ADDRESS...
....
....
....

TEL ....
FAX..
E-MAIL...

NAME...

ADDRESS...
....
....
....

TEL ....
FAX..
E-MAIL...

NAME...

ADDRESS...
....
....
....

TEL ....
FAX..
E-MAIL...

NAME...

ADDRESS...
....
....
....

TEL ....
FAX..
E-MAIL...

NAME...

ADDRESS...
....
....
....

TEL ....
FAX..
E-MAIL...

J

NAME..

ADDRESS...

....

....

TEL ....

FAX...

E-MAIL..

NAME..

ADDRESS...

....

....

TEL ....

FAX...

E-MAIL..

NAME..

ADDRESS...

....

....

TEL ....

FAX...

E-MAIL..

NAME..

ADDRESS...

....

....

TEL ....

FAX...

E-MAIL..

Oresto J. Toppi, *Sparring Airedales*, 1984

J

NAME...

ADDRESS...

....

....

....

TEL ....
FAX...
E-MAIL...

NAME...

ADDRESS...

....

....

....

TEL ....
FAX...
E-MAIL...

NAME...

ADDRESS...

....

....

....

TEL ....
FAX...
E-MAIL...

William Mackarness, Ch. Baby Ruth

NAME...

ADDRESS...

....

....

....

TEL ....
FAX...
E-MAIL...

Katherine S. Finch,
Int. Ch. Rudiki of Prides Hill, 1948

NAME...
....
ADDRESS..
....
....
....
TEL...
FAX..
E-MAIL...

NAME...
....
ADDRESS..
....
....
....
TEL...
FAX..
E-MAIL...

K

F.C. Clifton, *Fire Chief*, 1901

NAME...

ADDRESS...

....

....

....

TEL...

FAX...

E-MAIL...

NAME...

ADDRESS...

....

....

....

TEL...

FAX...

E-MAIL...

NAME...

ADDRESS...

....

....

....

TEL...

FAX...

E-MAIL...

NAME...

ADDRESS...

....

....

....

TEL...

FAX...

E-MAIL...

K

NAME..

ADDRESS...

....

....

TEL ....
FAX..
E-MAIL...

NAME..

ADDRESS...

....

....

TEL ....
FAX..
E-MAIL...

NAME..

ADDRESS...

....

....

TEL ....
FAX..
E-MAIL...

NAME..

ADDRESS...

....

....

TEL ....
FAX..
E-MAIL...

NAME..

ADDRESS...

....

....

TEL ....
FAX..
E-MAIL...

F.C. Clifton, *Ch. Yorkville Belle*, 1901

K

Kole Sowerby,
Don Leon, 1894

NAME...

ADDRESS...

....

....

....

TEL...

FAX..

E-MAIL..

NAME...

ADDRESS...

....

....

....

TEL...

FAX..

E-MAIL..

NAME..

ADDRESS...

....

....

TEL ....

FAX..

E-MAIL...

NAME..

ADDRESS...

....

....

TEL ....

FAX..

E-MAIL...

Kole Sowerby, *Bulldog*

NAME..

ADDRESS...

....

....

TEL ....

FAX..

E-MAIL...

NAME..

ADDRESS...

....

....

TEL ....

FAX..

E-MAIL...

L

NAME...
....
ADDRESS...
....
....
....
TEL...
FAX...
E-MAIL..

NAME...
....
ADDRESS...
....
....
....
TEL...
FAX...
E-MAIL..

NAME...
....
ADDRESS...
....
....
....
TEL...
FAX...
E-MAIL..

NAME...
....
ADDRESS...
....
....
....
TEL...
FAX...
E-MAIL..

NAME...
....
ADDRESS...
....
....
....
TEL...
FAX...
E-MAIL..

NAME...
....
ADDRESS...
....
....
....
TEL...
FAX...
E-MAIL..

NAME...
....
ADDRESS..
....
....
....
TEL ....
FAX...
E-MAIL..

NAME...
....
ADDRESS..
....
....
....
TEL ....
FAX...
E-MAIL..

F. Sinet, *Int. Ch. Seedley Sterling*, c.1916

NAME...
....
ADDRESS..
....
....
....
TEL ....
FAX...
E-MAIL..

NAME...
....
ADDRESS..
....
....
....
TEL ....
FAX...
E-MAIL..

L

NAME...

ADDRESS..
....
....
TEL...
FAX...
E-MAIL..

NAME...

ADDRESS..
....
....
TEL...
FAX...
E-MAIL..

NAME...

ADDRESS..
....
....
TEL...
FAX...
E-MAIL..

NAME...

ADDRESS..
....
....
TEL...
FAX...
E-MAIL..

NAME...

ADDRESS..
....
....
TEL...
FAX...
E-MAIL..

L

Left: George Earl, *Bob*, 1871

George W. Horlor,
What Will He Do with It?, 1882

NAME...

ADDRESS...

....

....

....

TEL...

FAX...

E-MAIL..

NAME...

ADDRESS...

....

....

....

TEL...

FAX...

E-MAIL..

M

NAME..

ADDRESS...

....

....

TEL ....

FAX..

E-MAIL...

NAME..

ADDRESS...

....

....

TEL ....

FAX..

E-MAIL...

NAME..

ADDRESS...

....

....

TEL ....

FAX..

E-MAIL...

NAME..

ADDRESS...

....

....

TEL ....

FAX..

E-MAIL...

Elkington & Co., *Hounds with Master of the Hunt*, 1896

M

NAME...

ADDRESS...

....

....

....

TEL...

FAX...

E-MAIL...

NAME...

ADDRESS...

....

....

....

TEL...

FAX...

E-MAIL...

NAME...

ADDRESS...

....

....

....

TEL...

FAX...

E-MAIL...

NAME...

ADDRESS...

....

....

....

TEL...

FAX...

E-MAIL...

NAME...

ADDRESS...

....

....

....

TEL...

FAX...

E-MAIL...

NAME...

ADDRESS...

....

....

....

TEL...

FAX...

E-MAIL...

William Giller after George W. Horlor,
A Group of Favorites

Right: Horatio Henry Coulde
Fox Terr.

NAME..

ADDRESS...

....

....

TEL..

FAX..

E-MAIL...

NAME..

ADDRESS...

....

....

TEL..

FAX..

E-MAIL...

NAME...

ADDRESS..

....

....

TEL ....
FAX..
E-MAIL...

NAME...

ADDRESS..

....

....

TEL ....
FAX..
E-MAIL...

NAME...

ADDRESS..

....

....

TEL ....
FAX..
E-MAIL...

NAME...

ADDRESS..

....

....

TEL ....
FAX..
E-MAIL...

M

NAME...
....
ADDRESS...
....
....
....
TEL ....
FAX...
E-MAIL..

NAME...
....
ADDRESS...
....
....
....
TEL ....
FAX...
E-MAIL..

NAME...
....
ADDRESS...
....
....
....
TEL ....
FAX...
E-MAIL..

NAME...
....
ADDRESS...
....
....
....
TEL ....
FAX...
E-MAIL..

NAME...
....
ADDRESS...
....
....
....
TEL ....
FAX...
E-MAIL..

NAME...
....
ADDRESS...
....
....
....
TEL ....
FAX...
E-MAIL..

John Martin Tracy, *Petrel*

NAME..

....

ADDRESS...

....

....

....

TEL...

FAX..

E-MAIL..

NAME..

....

ADDRESS...

....

....

....

TEL...

FAX..

E-MAIL..

N

NAME..

ADDRESS...

....

....

....

TEL ....

FAX...

E-MAIL..

NAME..

ADDRESS...

....

....

....

TEL ....

FAX...

E-MAIL..

N

NAME..

ADDRESS..

....

....

TEL..
FAX...
E-MAIL..

NAME..

ADDRESS..

....

....

TEL..
FAX...
E-MAIL..

Gustav Muss-Arnolt, *English Setter in the Field*

Left: John Martin Tracy, *Bob*

NAME..

ADDRESS..

....

....

TEL..
FAX...
E-MAIL..

NAME..

ADDRESS..

....

....

TEL..
FAX...
E-MAIL..

N

NAME..

ADDRESS..

....

....

....

TEL...
FAX...
E-MAIL...

NAME..

ADDRESS..

....

....

....

TEL...
FAX...
E-MAIL...

NAME..

ADDRESS..

....

....

....

TEL...
FAX...
E-MAIL...

NAME..

ADDRESS..

....

....

....

TEL...
FAX...
E-MAIL...

NAME..

ADDRESS..

....

....

....

TEL...
FAX...
E-MAIL...

NAME..
....
ADDRESS..
....
....
....
TEL..
FAX..
E-MAIL...

NAME..
....
ADDRESS..
....
....
....
TEL..
FAX..
E-MAIL...

Gustav Muss-Arnolt, *Tri-Color English Setter*

Left: Gustav Muss-Arnolt, *Beaufort*

NAME..
....
ADDRESS..
....
....
....
TEL..
FAX..
E-MAIL...

NAME..
....
ADDRESS..
....
....
....
TEL..
FAX..
E-MAIL...

N

NAME..

ADDRESS ....

....

....

TEL ....
FAX..
E-MAIL..

NAME..

ADDRESS ....

....

....

TEL ....
FAX..
E-MAIL..

Edmund Henry Osthaus,
Seven English Setters,
1911

Edmund Henry
Osthaus, *Toledo Blade*

NAME..	NAME..
....	....
ADDRESS..	ADDRESS..
....	....
....	....
....	....
TEL...	TEL...
FAX...	FAX...
E-MAIL..	E-MAIL..

O

NAME...

ADDRESS...

....

....

....

TEL ....
FAX...
E-MAIL..

NAME...

ADDRESS...

....

....

....

TEL ....
FAX...
E-MAIL..

NAME...

ADDRESS...

....

....

....

TEL ....
FAX...
E-MAIL..

NAME...

ADDRESS...

....

....

....

TEL ....
FAX...
E-MAIL..

NAME...

ADDRESS...

....

....

....

TEL ....
FAX...
E-MAIL..

NAME...

ADDRESS...

....

....

....

TEL ....
FAX...
E-MAIL..

O

Richard Fath, *Running Greyhounds*

P

NAME

ADDRESS

TEL

FAX

E-MAIL

NAME

ADDRESS

TEL

FAX

E-MAIL

NAME

ADDRESS

TEL

FAX

E-MAIL

NAME

ADDRESS

TEL

FAX

E-MAIL

NAME

ADDRESS

TEL

FAX

E-MAIL

P

NAME..

ADDRESS...

....

....

TEL...

FAX..

E-MAIL...

NAME..

ADDRESS...

....

....

TEL...

FAX..

E-MAIL...

S.G. Mapes, *Champion Wundah of Holly Lodge*, 1935

Left: Terri Bresnihan, *Fuh Sam*, 1939

NAME..

ADDRESS...

....

....

TEL...

FAX..

E-MAIL...

NAME..

ADDRESS...

....

....

TEL...

FAX..

E-MAIL...

P

NAME...

ADDRESS...

....

....

....

TEL ....
FAX..
E-MAIL..

NAME...

ADDRESS...

....

....

....

TEL ....
FAX..
E-MAIL..

NAME...

ADDRESS...

....

....

....

TEL ....
FAX..
E-MAIL..

NAME...

ADDRESS...

....

....

....

TEL ....
FAX..
E-MAIL..

NAME...

ADDRESS...

....

....

....

TEL ....
FAX..
E-MAIL..

NAME..

ADDRESS..

....

....

....

TEL ....

FAX..

E-MAIL..

NAME..

....

ADDRESS..

....

....

TEL ....

FAX..

E-MAIL..

Reuben Ward Binks, *Brigadier*, 1935

Left: Reuben Ward Binks, *Dawn and Day*, 1931

NAME..

ADDRESS..

....

....

....

TEL ....

FAX..

E-MAIL..

NAME..

....

ADDRESS..

....

....

TEL ....

FAX..

E-MAIL..

P

NAME..   NAME..
....
ADDRESS...   ADDRESS...
....
....
....
TEL ....   TEL ....
FAX...   FAX...
E-MAIL..   E-MAIL..

Left: Marguerite Kirmse,
Ch. Hemlock Hill Ivo Clyde, 1917

Marguerite Kirmse,
Ch. Hemlock Hill Boy Scout, 1918

NAME..

ADDRESS ....

....

....

TEL ....

FAX ....

E-MAIL ....

NAME..

ADDRESS ....

....

....

TEL ....

FAX ....

E-MAIL ....

Q

NAME..

ADDRESS..

....

....

TEL ....
FAX..
E-MAIL..

NAME..

ADDRESS..

....

....

TEL ....
FAX..
E-MAIL..

NAME..

ADDRESS..

....

....

TEL ....
FAX..
E-MAIL..

NAME..

ADDRESS..

....

....

TEL ....
FAX..
E-MAIL..

NAME..

ADDRESS..

....

....

TEL ....
FAX..
E-MAIL..

NAME..

ADDRESS..

....

....

TEL ....
FAX..
E-MAIL..

NAME..

....

ADDRESS ....

....

....

....

TEL ....

FAX...

E-MAIL..

Rosa Bonheur and Consuela Fould, *Rosa Bonheur*, 1896

NAME..

....

ADDRESS ....

....

....

....

TEL ....

FAX...

E-MAIL..

NAME..

....

ADDRESS ....

....

....

....

TEL ....

FAX...

E-MAIL..

NAME..

....

ADDRESS ....

....

....

....

TEL ....

FAX...

E-MAIL..

R

NAME..

ADDRESS..

....

....

TEL...
FAX...
E-MAIL..

NAME..

ADDRESS..

....

....

TEL...
FAX...
E-MAIL..

NAME..

ADDRESS..

....

....

TEL...
FAX...
E-MAIL..

NAME..

ADDRESS..

....

....

TEL...
FAX...
E-MAIL..

NAME..

ADDRESS..

....

....

TEL...
FAX...
E-MAIL..

Georges J.E. de Vuillefroy, *Full Cry*

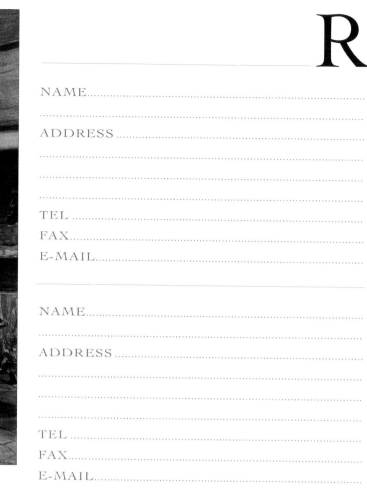

Charles Olivier de Penne, *Tricolor French Hounds*

R

NAME..

ADDRESS..

....

....

TEL..
FAX..
E-MAIL..

NAME..

ADDRESS..

....

....

TEL..
FAX..
E-MAIL..

NAME..

ADDRESS..

....

....

TEL..
FAX..
E-MAIL..

NAME..

ADDRESS..

....

....

TEL..
FAX..
E-MAIL..

R

NAME...

ADDRESS..

....

....

TEL...
FAX...
E-MAIL..

NAME...

ADDRESS..

....

....

TEL...
FAX...
E-MAIL..

NAME...

ADDRESS..

....

....

TEL...
FAX...
E-MAIL..

NAME...

ADDRESS..

....

....

TEL...
FAX...
E-MAIL..

NAME...

ADDRESS..

....

....

TEL...
FAX...
E-MAIL..

NAME...

ADDRESS..

....

....

TEL...
FAX...
E-MAIL..

NAME..

ADDRESS..

....

....

TEL ....

FAX..

E-MAIL...

NAME..

ADDRESS..

....

....

TEL ....

FAX..

E-MAIL...

Wilson Hepple, *Woman with Two Dogs*, 1882

NAME..

ADDRESS..

....

....

TEL ....

FAX..

E-MAIL...

NAME..

ADDRESS..

....

....

TEL ....

FAX..

E-MAIL...

R

NAME..
....
ADDRESS...
....
....
....
TEL...
FAX..
E-MAIL..

NAME..
....
ADDRESS...
....
....
....
TEL...
FAX..
E-MAIL..

NAME..
....
ADDRESS...
....
....
....
TEL...
FAX..
E-MAIL..

NAME..
....
ADDRESS...
....
....
....
TEL...
FAX..
E-MAIL..

NAME..
....
ADDRESS...
....
....
....
TEL...
FAX..
E-MAIL..

S

Left: Louis-Eugène Lambert,
Bichon Frise, 1854

Alfred de Dreux,
Innocence Between Two Friends

NAME..

ADDRESS..

....

....

....

TEL...

FAX...

E-MAIL..

NAME..

ADDRESS..

....

....

....

TEL...

FAX...

E-MAIL..

S

NAME...

ADDRESS...
....
....
....

TEL..
FAX...
E-MAIL...

NAME...

ADDRESS...
....
....
....

TEL..
FAX...
E-MAIL...

NAME...

ADDRESS...
....
....
....

TEL..
FAX...
E-MAIL...

NAME...

ADDRESS...
....
....
....

TEL..
FAX...
E-MAIL...

NAME...

ADDRESS...
....
....
....

TEL..
FAX...
E-MAIL...

NAME...

ADDRESS...
....
....
....

TEL..
FAX...
E-MAIL...

NAME...

ADDRESS ....

....

....

TEL ....

FAX...

E-MAIL...

NAME...

ADDRESS ....

....

....

TEL ....

FAX...

E-MAIL...

William Powell Frith, *Lady Flora Hastings with Horse and Dogs*

NAME...

ADDRESS ....

....

....

TEL ....

FAX..

E-MAIL...

NAME...

ADDRESS ....

....

....

TEL ....

FAX..

E-MAIL...

S

NAME..

ADDRESS..

....

....

TEL...
FAX...
E-MAIL...

NAME..

ADDRESS..

....

....

TEL...
FAX...
E-MAIL...

NAME..

ADDRESS..

....

....

TEL...
FAX...
E-MAIL...

NAME..

ADDRESS..

....

....

TEL...
FAX...
E-MAIL...

NAME..

ADDRESS..

....

....

TEL...
FAX...
E-MAIL...

S

Left: William Mangford after Edwin
Henry Landseer, *Odin*, 1872

After Edwin Henry Landseer,
Alexander and Diogenes

NAME...

....

ADDRESS..

....

....

....

TEL ....

FAX...

E-MAIL...

NAME...

....

ADDRESS..

....

....

....

TEL ....

FAX...

E-MAIL...

T

NAME...

ADDRESS...

....

....

....

TEL...
FAX...
E-MAIL..

NAME...

ADDRESS...

....

....

TEL...
FAX...
E-MAIL..

NAME...

ADDRESS...

....

....

TEL...
FAX...
E-MAIL..

NAME...

ADDRESS...

....

....

TEL...
FAX...
E-MAIL..

NAME...

ADDRESS...

....

....

TEL...
FAX...
E-MAIL..

NAME...

ADDRESS...

....

....

TEL...
FAX...
E-MAIL..

NAME..

ADDRESS...

....

....

....

TEL..
FAX..
E-MAIL..

NAME..

ADDRESS...

....

....

....

TEL..
FAX..
E-MAIL..

NAME..

ADDRESS...

....

....

....

TEL..
FAX..
E-MAIL..

NAME..

ADDRESS...

....

....

....

TEL..
FAX..
E-MAIL..

After Edwin Henry Landseer, *The Connoisseurs*, 1867

T

NAME...

ADDRESS..

....

....

TEL..
FAX...
E-MAIL..

NAME...

ADDRESS..

....

....

TEL..
FAX...
E-MAIL..

NAME...

ADDRESS..

....

....

TEL..
FAX...
E-MAIL..

NAME...

ADDRESS..

....

....

TEL..
FAX...
E-MAIL..

NAME...

ADDRESS..

....

....

TEL..
FAX...
E-MAIL..

Charles Hamilton, *Zillah*

NAME..

ADDRESS..

....

....

TEL..
FAX...
E-MAIL...

NAME..

ADDRESS..

....

....

TEL..
FAX...
E-MAIL...

NAME..

ADDRESS..

....

....

TEL..
FAX...
E-MAIL...

NAME..

ADDRESS..

....

....

TEL..
FAX...
E-MAIL...

NAME..

ADDRESS..

....

....

TEL..
FAX...
E-MAIL...

James Ward, *Salukis*

T

NAME...

ADDRESS...
....
....

TEL...
FAX...
E-MAIL...

NAME...

ADDRESS...
....
....

TEL...
FAX...
E-MAIL...

NAME...

ADDRESS...
....
....

TEL...
FAX...
E-MAIL...

NAME...

ADDRESS...
....
....

TEL...
FAX...
E-MAIL...

NAME...

ADDRESS...
....
....

TEL...
FAX...
E-MAIL...

NAME...

ADDRESS...
....
....

TEL...
FAX...
E-MAIL...

NAME...
....
ADDRESS...
....
....
TEL ....
FAX...
E-MAIL...

NAME...
....
ADDRESS...
....
....
TEL ....
FAX...
E-MAIL...

NAME...
....
ADDRESS...
....
....
TEL ....
FAX...
E-MAIL...

Richard Cosway, *Master Thomas Thornhill*

U

NAME..

ADDRESS...

....

....

TEL ....
FAX...
E-MAIL...

NAME..

ADDRESS...

....

....

TEL ....
FAX...
E-MAIL...

NAME..

ADDRESS...

....

....

TEL ....
FAX...
E-MAIL...

NAME..

ADDRESS...

....

....

TEL ....
FAX...
E-MAIL...

Left: Carl Reichert, *French Bulldog*, 1874

Conradijn Cunaeus, *Scottish Deerhounds in an Interior*

NAME..

ADDRESS...

....

....

....

TEL...

FAX...

E-MAIL...

NAME..

ADDRESS...

....

....

....

TEL...

FAX...

E-MAIL...

V

NAME..

ADDRESS ....

....

....

....

TEL ....

FAX..

E-MAIL..

NAME..

ADDRESS ....

....

....

....

TEL ....

FAX..

E-MAIL..

NAME..

ADDRESS ....

....

....

....

TEL ....

FAX..

E-MAIL..

NAME..

ADDRESS ....

....

....

....

TEL ....

FAX..

E-MAIL..

Henry Thomas Alken, Sr., *Dog Outside Kennel with Terrier*

NAME..

ADDRESS ....

....

....

....

TEL ....

FAX..

E-MAIL..

V

Henry Birche after George Stubbs, *The Game Keepers*, 1790

NAME...

....

ADDRESS...

....

....

....

TEL ....

FAX ....

E-MAIL ....

NAME...

....

ADDRESS...

....

....

....

TEL ....

FAX ....

E-MAIL ....

NAME...

....

ADDRESS...

....

....

....

TEL ....

FAX ....

E-MAIL ....

NAME...

....

ADDRESS...

....

....

....

TEL ....

FAX ....

E-MAIL ....

NAME...

....

ADDRESS...

....

....

....

TEL ....

FAX ....

E-MAIL ....

V

John Martin Tracy,
Open Season

NAME..	NAME..
....	....
ADDRESS...	ADDRESS...
....	....
....	....
....	....
TEL..	TEL..
FAX..	FAX..
E-MAIL...	E-MAIL...

W

NAME...

ADDRESS..

....

....

....

TEL..
FAX..
E-MAIL..

NAME...

ADDRESS..

....

....

....

TEL..
FAX..
E-MAIL..

NAME...

ADDRESS..

....

....

....

TEL..
FAX..
E-MAIL..

NAME...

ADDRESS..

....

....

....

TEL..
FAX..
E-MAIL..

NAME...

ADDRESS..

....

....

....

TEL..
FAX..
E-MAIL..

NAME...

ADDRESS..

....

....

....

TEL..
FAX..
E-MAIL..

W

NAME..

ADDRESS...

....

....

TEL..

FAX..

E-MAIL..

NAME..

ADDRESS...

....

....

TEL..

FAX..

E-MAIL..

NAME..

ADDRESS...

....

....

TEL..

FAX..

E-MAIL..

NAME..

ADDRESS...

....

....

TEL..

FAX..

E-MAIL..

Left: Alfred Duke,
Terrier and Rabbit

Edwin Megargee,
For Sale, Setter Puppies

NAME.. NAME..

....

ADDRESS.. ADDRESS..

....

....

....

TEL... TEL...

FAX... FAX...

E-MAIL.. E-MAIL..

W

NAME...

ADDRESS...

....

....

....

TEL...

FAX...

E-MAIL...

NAME...

ADDRESS...

....

....

....

TEL...

FAX...

E-MAIL...

NAME...

ADDRESS...

....

....

....

TEL...

FAX...

E-MAIL...

NAME...

ADDRESS...

....

....

....

TEL...

FAX...

E-MAIL...

NAME...

ADDRESS...

....

....

....

TEL...

FAX...

E-MAIL...

NAME...

ADDRESS...

....

....

....

TEL...

FAX...

E-MAIL...

Edwin Megargee, *Ch. Bonnie Brighteyes of Mannerhead and Blakeen and Ch. Arnim of Piperscroft, 1937*

NAME..

....

ADDRESS..

....

....

....

TEL...

FAX..

E-MAIL...

NAME..

....

ADDRESS..

....

....

....

TEL...

FAX..

E-MAIL...

W

NAME..

ADDRESS...

....

....

TEL...
FAX...
E-MAIL..

NAME..

ADDRESS...

....

....

....

TEL...
FAX...
E-MAIL..

NAME..

ADDRESS...

....

....

TEL...
FAX...
E-MAIL..

NAME..

ADDRESS...

....

....

TEL...
FAX...
E-MAIL..

X

NAME...

ADDRESS...

....

....

TEL ....

FAX...

E-MAIL..

NAME...

ADDRESS...

....

....

TEL ....

FAX...

E-MAIL..

NAME...

ADDRESS...

....

....

TEL ....

FAX...

E-MAIL..

J. Alden Weir, *Words of Comfort*, 1887

Left: A.-V.-A. Boudarel, *Mastiff with a French Bulldog*

X

NAME...
....
ADDRESS...
....
....
....
TEL ....
FAX...
E-MAIL...

NAME...
....
ADDRESS...
....
....
....
TEL ....
FAX...
E-MAIL...

NAME...
....
ADDRESS...
....
....
....
TEL ....
FAX...
E-MAIL...

NAME...
....
ADDRESS...
....
....
....
TEL ....
FAX...
E-MAIL...

NAME...
....
ADDRESS...
....
....
....
TEL ....
FAX...
E-MAIL...

NAME...
....
ADDRESS...
....
....
....
TEL ....
FAX...
E-MAIL...

NAME..

ADDRESS...

....

....

TEL...
FAX...
E-MAIL...

NAME..

ADDRESS...

....

....

TEL...
FAX...
E-MAIL...

NAME..

ADDRESS...

....

....

TEL...
FAX...
E-MAIL...

NAME..

ADDRESS...

....

....

TEL...
FAX...
E-MAIL...

NAME..

ADDRESS...

....

....

TEL...
FAX...
E-MAIL...

Damara Bolté, *Ch. Oak Tree's Irishtocrat, C.D.*

Z

NAME...

ADDRESS...

....

....

TEL ....
FAX...
E-MAIL...

NAME...

ADDRESS...

....

....

TEL ....
FAX...
E-MAIL...

NAME...

ADDRESS...

....

....

TEL ....
FAX...
E-MAIL...

NAME...

ADDRESS...

....

....

TEL ....
FAX...
E-MAIL...

NAME...

ADDRESS...

....

....

TEL ....
FAX...
E-MAIL...

NAME...

ADDRESS...

....

....

TEL ....
FAX...
E-MAIL...

Kathy Jakobsen, *Dog Walking in Central Park*, 1993